It's OK to Cry

MOLLY POTTER

ILLUSTRATED BY SARAH JENNINGS

BLOOMSBURY EDUCATION

LONDON OXFORD NEW YORK NEW DELHI SYDNEY

Dedicated to my husband Andy who, like many of his age, was taught to keep his feelings very well hidden.
(But don't worry – it's being worked on!)

BLOOMSBURY EDUCATION
Bloomsbury Publishing Plc
50 Bedford Square, London, WC1B 3DP, UK
29 Earlsfort Terrace, Dublin 2, Ireland
BLOOMSBURY, BLOOMSBURY EDUCATION and the Diana logo are trademarks of Bloomsbury Publishing Plc
First published in Great Britain, 2020 by Bloomsbury Publishing Plc
This edition published in Great Britain, 2024 by Bloomsbury Publishing Plc
Text copyright © Molly Potter, 2020
Illustrations copyright © Sarah Jennings, 2020

A catalogue record for this book is available from the British Library

ISBN: HB: 978-1-4729-4242-5; PB: 978-1-8019-9433-0; ePDF: 978-1-4729-4241-8; ePUB: 978-1-4729-7719-9

2 4 6 8 10 9 7 5 3 1 (hardback)
2 4 6 8 10 9 7 5 3 1 (paperback)

Printed and bound in China by RR Donnelley Asia Printing Company Ltd, Dongguan, Guangdong

To find out more about our authors and books visit www.bloomsbury.com and sign up for our newsletters

It's OK to Cry

This book is called *It's OK to Cry* for a reason. It really is OK to cry! Everyone needs to be able to express how they feel and what makes them feel that way. When you get good at understanding your emotions and being able to talk about them openly, it can stop you from hurting people in the heat of the moment, it can make you feel better and it means you'll have a better chance of getting the help you need.

This book starts off exploring why boys in particular tend to struggle with their emotions and find it hard to express their feelings. It then looks at different emotions in turn and when you might experience them. It will help you explain to other people exactly how you are feeling and why. It will also help you understand how to get better at coping with and responding to uncomfortable feelings. Getting better at dealing with feelings will make your life a whole lot easier!

It's good to know...

People nearly always feel better after a good cry.

Contents

NOTES FOR PARENTS AND CARERS

Why do some boys hide their emotions?

Boys often hear things that can make them believe:

They have to be tough.

Stop making such a fuss.

They have to learn to cope on their own.

Go on in, you'll be fine on your own.

Can you come in with me?

They need to be strong.

That boy just hurt me.

You need to stand up for yourself.

The only feeling they should show is anger because it's powerful.

I hate getting told off!

Boys can also end up thinking:

They need to be in control.

Freddie said I couldn't play football with him.

Tell him you're in charge and he can't stop you.

They must be brave.

Go on, don't be such a sissy!

It's only OK for girls to talk about their feelings.

I feel miserable.

I've never heard a boy say he's miserable before.

They are not supposed to cry.

Come on, crying is just for girls.

So what does all this mean?

Because of messages like the ones on this page, boys can end up feeling they can't talk about or show their feelings and that they have to deal with problems on their own. This is really unfair as boys can still feel scared, nervous, upset, worried, helpless, insecure and sad. Sharing feelings is a positive thing and can make you feel less alone with your worries.

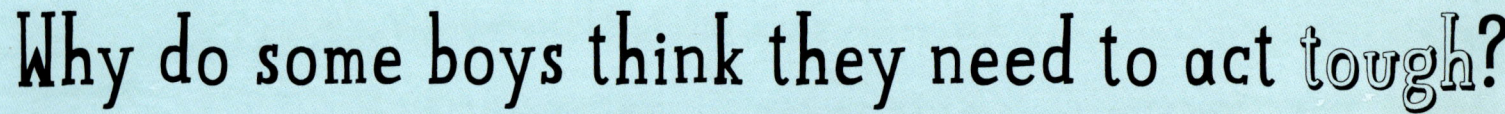

Why do some boys think they need to act tough?

Many boys are told over and over again that they need to be tough. They pick this up from adverts on TV, from watching action films, from reading stories with male heroes who never cry and from some of the adults in their lives.

How many messages that encourage boys to be tough can you see in this picture?

Be brave, don't cry.

It's good to know...

Sadly, boys are often taught that part of being tough includes not talking about their feelings. This is really unhelpful.

Why it's good to talk about feelings

Life is a lot easier if you can talk to other people about the things that are bothering you. If you manage to talk about difficult feelings and what made you feel that way, you'll start to feel better and you'll be more likely to get the help you need.

I'm really worried about getting a new teacher.

I feel lonely at play times.

I feel scared when there's thunder and lightning.

I'm feeling upset because my mum and dad had a big argument this morning.

I'm feeling sad because my grandad can't visit me now.

The following pages give you lots of words for feelings and suggest times when you might feel that way. Thinking about these words and situations can help you get better at expressing how you feel.

Positive feelings that can make you smile

Some feelings can make you think that everything in life is great. Here are some feelings that are just like that.

Feeling EXCITED the night before your birthday.

Feeling AMUSED when someone tells you a joke.

Knock, knock!

Feeling PROUD when you score a goal in a football match.

Feeling DELIGHTED when you open a present and realise it's exactly what you wanted.

Feeling AMAZED when you learn to ride a bike for the first time.

Feeling HAPPY having a picnic with your family and it's all your favourite food.

Feeling PLEASED when someone admires your new boots.

Feeling ENTHUSIASTIC when you're doing something you absolutely love doing.

It's good to know...

Positive feelings are great and everyone likes to have them. When you feel like this it's wonderful but nobody can feel this way all of the time.

Negative feelings that can make you frown

Some negative feelings can make you feel really cross. These feelings can sometimes make you want to stomp around and shout!

Feeling ANNOYED when someone is making a noise in your ear and you're trying to listen to something else.

Ping, pong, gazza, plop, whizz!

Feeling ANGRY when someone hurts or upsets you on purpose.

Feeling IRRITATED when every time you go to draw a picture, your pencil breaks.

Feeling DISGUSTED when you discover dog poo on your shoe.

Feeling FURIOUS when someone makes you really, really angry.

Not again!

Feeling FRUSTRATED when you keep trying to do something but don't manage it.

Leave her alone!

Feeling ENRAGED when someone you really care about gets teased.

Feeling GRUMPY when you have to stay indoors all day and you were looking forward to going to the park.

It's good to know...

If you don't stop and think about the best way to deal with the feelings described on this page, they can make you do things that upset other people.

Feelings that can take over and are not at all enjoyable

The feelings on these pages can be quite powerful as they can take over your thoughts and make you feel all wobbly inside.

Feeling WORRIED when you think something awful is going to happen and you won't be able to cope.

Feeling INSECURE when you don't feel confident about how something is going to turn out.

Feeling SCARED when you believe something could hurt or harm you.

Feeling PETRIFIED when you're really, really scared.

Feeling ANXIOUS when you worry a lot about how something is going to turn out.

I thought that would make it better.

I'm really worried I'll let lots of goals in tomorrow.

Feeling HELPLESS when you think there is nothing anyone can do to make things better.

Feeling INTIMIDATED when someone scares you on purpose to try and get you to do what they want.

Feeling OVERWHELMED when there are too many things happening at once and you're not sure what to do first.

It's good to know...

When you feel these feelings, one of the best things you can do is find someone you trust to talk to about what's bothering you. This can make you feel better.

Feelings that can make you cry

These feelings are the opposite of being happy. Although we don't enjoy these emotions, everyone should expect to feel them now and again.

Feeling UPSET when a toy you love gets broken.

I loved this robot.

Feeling DISAPPOINTED when you can no longer go on an outing you were really looking forward to.

I'm sorry sweetheart, you can't go to the fair.

Feeling HURT when someone you really like says something horrible to you.

That's rubbish!

Feeling SAD when you have to say goodbye to someone you love that you might not see for a while.

See you next year.

Feeling MISERABLE
when a pet dies.

I'll really miss Squiggles.

Feeling REGRET when you've done something you wish you hadn't done.

It's very clear you copied her.

Feeling HOPELESS when you believe things are so awful, you can't imagine they will ever get better.

Feeling DISTRESSED when you are lost in a place you don't know.

I can't see my dad anywhere!

It's good to know...

When you have these feelings, sometimes a good cry can make you feel much better.

Feelings that involve other people

There are some emotions you only feel because of other people – what they do or say or things they own make you feel certain ways.

Feeling EMBARRASSED when others notice you've done something a bit silly.

I feel really left out.

Feeling JEALOUS when a good friend spends more time with someone else than with you.

Feeling SHY when you meet lots of people you don't know.

Feeling SYMPATHETIC when something bad happens to someone you care about.

Feeling PITY when you're upset about something bad that has happened to someone else.

Feeling MISUNDERSTOOD when someone hasn't listened to your side of the story.

Feeling HATRED when you really don't like someone.

Feeling IMPRESSED when a friend does something really amazing.

It's good to know...

People sometimes do things that cause you to have really strong emotions. This is probably because people are designed to care about other people and what they think and feel.

Feelings that show you care

If we care for other people, when we spend time with them or think about them, we feel a warm glow inside but part of caring also means we feel sad when they feel sad.

Feeling LOVE when you really care about someone and enjoy being with them.

Feeling AFFECTIONATE when you are enjoying the love you feel for someone.

Feeling EMPATHY when you can imagine how someone else is feeling.

Feeling CONCERN when you care about someone who is having a difficult time.

It's good to know...

The people we feel closest to tend to bring out the strongest feelings in us that are both enjoyable and unenjoyable. This is all part of caring about others.

Quiet feelings

These feelings tend not to make you jump about and shout 'yippee' as they are gently enjoyable.

Feeling CALM when absolutely nothing is bothering you.

Feeling CONTENT when you are calm and happy and don't think you need anything.

Feeling RELAXED when you don't have a lot to do and you're enjoying yourself.

Feeling RELIEVED when something that was worrying you turns out to be OK.

It's good to know...

The feelings on this page are good for us and can help keep our minds and bodies healthy.

Feelings you have because of what you're thinking

What you think affects how you feel and how you feel can affect what you think. Thoughts and feelings are linked.

Thank you so much, that's my favourite.

I have the best mummy.

It's scary but I can do this.

Feeling BRAVE when you decide you will have a go at something that scares you.

Feeling GRATEFUL when you think you're lucky because of something you've been given or something you have that's special.

Feeling HOPEFUL when you take part in a drawing competition and you think you have a chance of winning.

Feeling TRUSTFUL when you know someone who will never let you down. They will always keep you safe and not upset you deliberately.

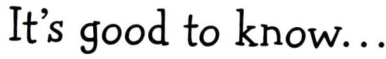

It's good to know...

When you spend time thinking about all the good things in your life, this can actually affect how you're feeling in a good way.

Feelings that can make you ask questions

These feelings can make you wonder and feel the need for more information.

Feeling INTERESTED when something has got your attention.

Feeling CONFUSED when you can't understand something so you don't know what you're meant to do.

Feeling SURPRISED when something you were not expecting happens.

Feeling CURIOUS when you really want to know more.

It's good to know...

Some feelings leave you wanting to know more information. When this happens, be sure to ask questions as the answers should be interesting or help you.

Feelings that can bother you a lot

These feelings can make your tummy feel tight, make you go quiet and make you feel uncomfortable. They are feelings nobody enjoys.

Feeling REJECTED when someone tells you they don't want to play with you.

Feeling GUILTY when you break something that doesn't belong to you.

Feeling ENVIOUS when someone else has got something you've always really wanted.

Feeling ASHAMED when you've done something bad and someone makes you understand it was wrong.

24

Feeling SHOCKED when someone surprises you – usually with something bad.

Feeling NERVOUS when you have to perform in front of other people.

Feeling TENSE when you just can't relax.

Feeling STRESSED when you've got more to cope with than you think you can handle. (Grown-ups tend to say they are stressed more than children.)

It's good to know...

Everyone finds different ways of coping with difficult feelings. Some ways of coping include: finding a way to relax, thinking about what happened in a way that makes it seem less important and, of course, talking to someone you trust to see if there is anything that can be done to help.

A park full of feelings

Each child on this page is labelled with what they are feeling. Can you say why you think they are feeling that way?

EXCITED

DISTRACTED

BORED

HUMILIATED

SATISFIED

ASTONISHED

Wow!

HAPPY

Steps you can take to help you deal with *uncomfortable* feelings

Am I feeling disappointed, frustrated or furious?

Step 1:

STOP and take time to think.

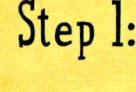

Step 2:

Try and put a name to the emotion you're feeling.

Step 3:

Work out what it was that triggered you to feel that way.

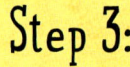

My friend said he can't come to my party.

Step 4:

Think about what is the best thing to do to help you cope with that emotion.

I'm going to think about all the people who are coming to my party and how much fun it will be.

Things you can do to help you cope with uncomfortable feelings

Find someone you trust to talk to about what has happened.

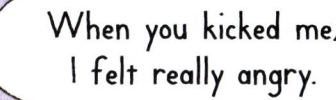

When you kicked me, I felt really angry.

If you feel that way because of something someone did, tell them how you feel.

Close your eyes, take some deep breaths and imagine yourself doing something you really enjoy.

I have to remember everyone makes mistakes.

When you can, stop any unhelpful thoughts and replace them with helpful ones.

It's good to know...

Something that can help you understand emotions even better is to wonder what other people might be feeling. You can do this by looking at their face, listening to what they're saying and how they're saying it and thinking about what might have just happened to them.

Notes for parents and carers

Helping boys become emotionally intelligent

There is a tendency for boys to perceive that showing any emotion other than anger is not acceptable. Even if as a parent/carer you try hard to encourage your son to express his emotions, as he grows up he will still be exposed to the idea that boys have to be tough and self-reliant.

This comes from a variety of sources such as films, adverts and other males in their lives. Because of this, boys are likely to suppress their emotions. This doesn't mean they are not experiencing them, it just means they are not expressing them.

Over time, a boy might learn to keep his emotions bottled up inside, until occasions when they become too much and bubble over, usually in the form of aggression. Anger shown as aggression is, of course, perceived as acceptable because it's powerful, strong and one of the emotions that can make us feel in control or dominant.

The impact of bottling up feelings, needing to appear to be in control and to be self-reliant can have a detrimental effect on a boy's ability to access help, form healthy relationships and develop healthy coping strategies at difficult times. In the more extreme cases, poor male emotional literacy is reflected in the fact that suicide is the single biggest cause of death for men under the age of 45 in the UK. Years of discouraging boys from exploring their emotions has undoubtedly done them no favours.

When a boy is experiencing a negative emotion, try really hard not to use phrases like:

• Be a brave boy.
• What's all this fuss about?
• Don't be so soppy.
• Boys don't cry.

As your child's parent/carer, you can have a very positive impact on how your child processes emotions. Here is some advice to help you do this:

Help your child understand that all emotions are just part of being human and they can't be avoided.
Explain that some emotions feel comfortable (being happy, relaxed) and some feel uncomfortable (being sad, angry, worried), some feel weak and some feel strong. Also explain that nobody can feel positive emotions, such as happiness, all the time.

Acknowledge feelings as often as you can in both yourself and your child.
Never negate what your child is feeling even if it seems like an exaggerated response to what happened. Emotions can be very strong and whatever your child is feeling is very real for them. Use phrases like, 'I'd be sad too if that happened to me' or 'I'm wondering if you are angry because…'

When your child is experiencing an emotion, ask them to name what they are feeling.
Ask them to describe *where* they can feel it in their body so they become better at acknowledging and recognising different emotions. Ask them to identify what made them feel that way to help them link cause and effect. Do this for both positive and negative feelings.

Help your child to imagine what others might be feeling (developing empathy).
Discuss how they think someone would feel in different scenarios, in stories you read to them or in real life situations that they witness.

With uncomfortable feelings, help your child put a gap between what they are feeling and their response to help them make better choices when they are experiencing a strong emotion.
It takes practice to do this – especially for those for whom the 'red mist' descends rapidly. In this gap, you can help your child to:

* Focus on what their body feels like.

* Put a name to what they are feeling.

* Be curious about anyone else involved, e.g. what might have made them do what they did. Instead of thinking, 'I'm going to say something nasty back,' consider, 'Maybe they are just having a really difficult day,' or 'Maybe I did something to upset them.'

* Consider what they could do that would not cause harm, e.g. walk away, breathe deeply, go and talk to someone.

* Consider what triggered the emotion.

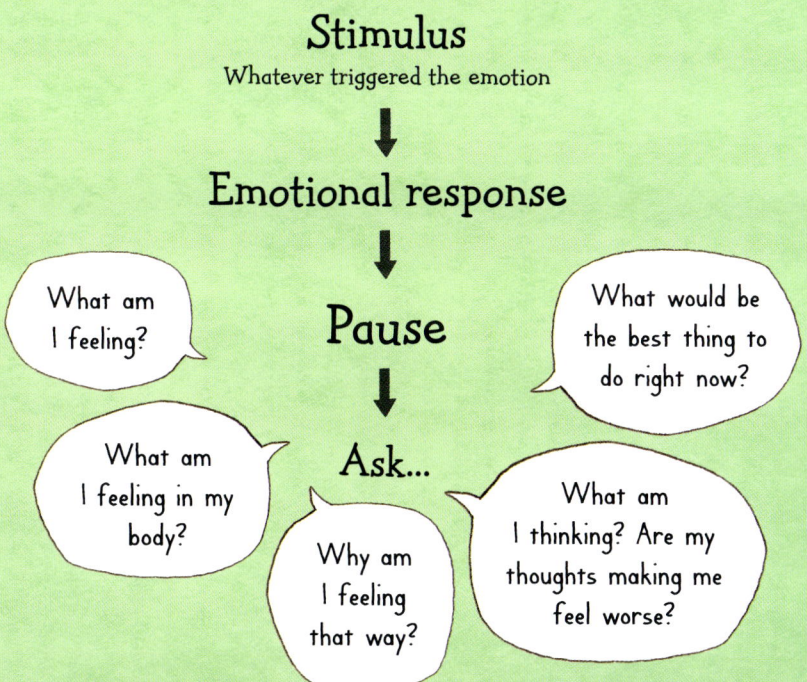

Stimulus
Whatever triggered the emotion
↓
Emotional response
↓
Pause
↓
Ask...

What am I feeling?

What would be the best thing to do right now?

What am I feeling in my body?

Why am I feeling that way?

What am I thinking? Are my thoughts making me feel worse?

Help your child develop healthy coping strategies for dealing with uncomfortable feelings that can include:

* Understanding that when they are feeling a strong emotion, their thinking brain is not working very well. Explain that they can engage the thinking brain only after the emotion has 'cooled down'. Then they can consider if there's anything practical that could be done to help the situation.

* Seeing a situation with a different perspective, e.g. things feel better after some time has passed. Help your child to visualise the situation as tiny, being kicked out of the window or locked up in a box, or to see the situation from another person's viewpoint.

* Letting go of things they can do nothing about.

* Learning calming activities, e.g. relaxation through music.

* Exploring meditation and mindfulness. Start by getting your child to concentrate on their breathing, or doing a body scan where they consider the sensations in the different parts of their body.

* Being optimistic about what happened. Ask your child, 'Did you learn anything or was there anything good about the situation?'

* Always encouraging your child to talk to you or someone they trust about what is bothering them.

How would you feel?

Describe how you think you would feel if...

One of your favourite people was coming to visit but you've just heard they can no longer come.

You've just found out you've won a colouring competition with a great prize.

You're trying to cross the road when a car drives past you really fast and toots its horn.

You've been told there is a surprise waiting for you when you get home.

Your friend had just told you they are going on holiday and will be swimming with dolphins.

You stand up in front of everyone to say a line in a play but you can't remember the line.

You get teased about the shoes you're wearing.

You're trying to build a model of a dinosaur but there's glue everywhere and everything is getting sticky and messy.

A friend pushed you and then laughed.

You got told off for something you didn't do.

You've just learnt to juggle with five balls.